A Basket of Roses:
Standing in My Shoes

Tatiana Whigham

Copyright © 2016. All rights reserved.

No part of this publication may be reproduced, stored in a retrieval system or transmitted in any way by any means, electronic, mechanical, photocopy, recording or otherwise, without the prior permission of the author except as provided by USA copyright law.

All characters appearing in this work are fictitious. Any resemblance to real persons, living or dead, is purely coincidental.

The opinions expressed by the author are not necessarily those of Revival Waves of Glory Books & Publishing.

Published by Revival Waves of Glory Books & Publishing

PO Box 596| Litchfield, Illinois 62056 USA

www.revivalwavesofgloryministries.com

Revival Waves of Glory Books & Publishing is committed to excellence in the publishing industry.

Book design Copyright © 2016 by Revival Waves of Glory Books & Publishing. All rights reserved.

Published in the United States of America

Paperback: 978-1-68411-108-4

Dedication

This book is dedicated to the late Evangelist, a man whose shoes were hard to fill. There's no beauty in life without pain. Soar high. . . .soar high!

Contents

Introduction: 1

Chapter 1: 4

Chapter 2: 13

Chapter 3: 18

Chapter 4: 24

Chapter 5: 39

Chapter 6: 47

Chapter 7: 58

Chapter 8: 67

Introduction:
April 1, 2015

Momma Dee

Twiddling my fingers like I'm the last Girl Scout or something, I sit patiently waiting in my seat. See that's how all of these high-priced doctors get you. They make you schedule appointments way in advance, sign you in, and then show up late themselves. I took a whole hour off this morning just so that I would be on time, and when I get here, he's late.

Sitting impatiently in my seat, I can't help but think that I have a hundred things to do today. I have to pick up both Tammie and the boys from school, help them with their homework, start dinner, get them ready for bed, and I still have to work the graveyard shift tonight. Getting a nap is out of the question, especially if I don't leave here pretty soon.

In the midst of my thoughts, the door opens. Thank you Lord! It's about time. "Well, we have the lab results back." In walks Dr. Taylor as he finds a seat of his own.

"Well?" come on, are you going to tell me or what? I've been waiting here just about 40 minutes, and I don't have all day.

Taking a sip of his coffee before continuing, "I don't see any progress. We've been treating this as best we know how and nothing seems to be working." Taking a deep sigh, he continues. "I think that you should consider alternatives."

"Alternatives? Like what?"

"Like rest for one? Look at you, you're getting up in age and you're still pushing anywhere between 40-50 hours a week working. With your health and your condition, it makes no sense to keep treating you if you refuse to rest your body long enough to let the treatment take effect."

"Well, . . ." shifting in my seat. "I can . . .probably take a day or two off."

"I'm not talking about a few days. . ." pulling his chair closer to me now. "I'm talking about a few years. . . maybe even permanently."

Feeling his words hit me like a ton of bricks, my eyes fill up with tears of suppressed hope. "You know I can't do that. . . .I've got my children and my grands depending on me to—"

"If you don't take some time off, . . . they won't be depending on you. They'll be burying you!" backing up in his seat and heading for the door with his charts. He stops just short of the door, "With you pushing yourself the way that you are, your body won't hold up too much longer. . . .I give you two, maybe three months tops."

Gasping for air, I grab my chest, trying to save the last little bit of life still within me. Gathering my thoughts, I look at him with boldness, "God has the last say so."

Laughing a little to himself, he replies back "That He does. . . Let's hope that He's on our side on this one." And with that, he walks out, leaving me to comfort myself. Oh Lord, . . . Oh my Lord!

Chapter 1:
April 12, 2015

Momma Dee

Sometimes, I believe that joy and sadness are seeds of love, because you can never have one without the other. Standing here in my kitchen, my mind falls back to when I was a little girl and life was carefree. How ignorant I was? But yet and still, my mother bore with me. She understood that I had yet learned about life, and I think that's why she always had so many tears in her eyes. She loved me too much to let the pain show; I didn't understand it then, but I know now. So today, I stand here with my soul so heavy. With nothing else left, I sing, because that's all that is left in me. Starting first with a hum, and then with a trickle of a sound, my whole life is summed up in this moment to be song a loud.

"If I had wings, I'd fly away. If I had wings, I'd fly away. If I had wings, I'd fly away from down here. Oh Lord, I would pick up my cross, put it on my shoulder, lift up wings, and fly home to glory. Wings, wings, wings . . . I sure wouldn't be down here—"

"Momma Dee, what are you singing?" startled, I turn back to see Tammie, my baby girl. Watching her walk in all groggy with bags underneath her eyes, it's clear that waking up is the last thing that she wants to do this morning.

Stumbling to the table, she looks up at me, anxiously waiting for breakfast. Still stirring the grits, I just smile.

"That's just some old song that my momma used to sing on days like this."

"What days? Sunday mornings? . . . Grandma, that ain't no 'Jesus Loves Me.'" Oh my Lord, this here child sure is a character. Laughing somewhat to myself, I can't do anything but look at her. My poor baby,. . . . my poor baby.

"Well. . . .since you think that about my song, why don't you sing one sweetie? Something that'll make this old lady smile, you hear."

"Oh Momma Dee, I don't think that I can sing anything this morning. I'm not up yet like I should be."

"Really? Because it seems to me like you've stayed up late last night watching TV."

Not really wanting to admit it, she just shifts uncomfortably in her seat. "Momma Dee, I'm 12 years-old. And in just about two months, I'll be 13 which would make me a teenager."

"And you're point is?"

"Why do I have to be the only teenager on the block to have a bed-time on the weekend?" just looking at her, my blood runs hot. I promise you, when these children get to be a certain age and start to smell themselves, Jesus Himself can't reason with them.

"Because you're the only teenager that lives on 501 Franklin Drive. Now don't you forget it." Watching her fold her arms, I can just tell that she has a mouthful of sly thoughts still brewing, but luckily she's not dumb enough to say them at the moment. Thank the Lord for that.

Turning back to my grits still steaming on the stove, I feel just as faint as I want to be. But with six kids in the house, who's going to do this if I don't? Shoot, it feels like I have everybody piling up in here like it's some kind of free room and board or something. There's Sonya (whose 34 and already twice divorced) and her two boys (Tyrell and Zectric), Lamar (who's 26 years old, and still can't seem to find a stable job), Bridgett (who's pushing 21), and Tammie. Momma told me that I should've waited to have children later on in life, but the good Lord said otherwise. Now here I am, pushing 50 and still have to work two jobs, because my children aren't stable enough to carry their own weight. Maybe I breastfeed them too long. Maybe I sheltered them from too much. Maybe I just didn't push them enough, because none of them, and I mean not one of them is doing anything with their life right now. Taking a deep breath, I have to contain myself, at least in front of Tammie. She doesn't need to be exposed to all of this. With no other way to vent, I just start back singing.

"If I had wings, I'd fly away. If I had wings, I'd fly away. If I had wings, I'd—"

"Oh good Lord momma, will you give that song a rest already." Turning around, it's Bridgett who from the looks of things just walked through the door. As a baby, I nick-named her Bridgee, because she was the only bridge that held me and my poor Robert together. Humph, how dumb was I to even think that a baby could hold a man? But we live and we learn. When she was younger, she was a spitting image of me, and up until this day, she still is. And I don't just mean the looks either. No Lord, she's got my attitude, my temper, my ways. . . .my everything. It's like watching a play by play some odd 20 years later, but momma told me that I'd get it back someday. Moving to the oven to check the biscuits, I try my best to keep calm, not really wanting to say anything that we both would regret.

"And where have you been?" turning to her now.

"Ok momma, get a grip. I'm not Tammie alright. I'm grown and I can do what I want to do."

"Not as long as you're in my house! If you want to do your own thing, then get out and get your own place."

Coming closer to the table now, "Ha! Ha! Are you serious right now? This ain't even your house! This is Grandma's house. Taking about I got to leave. I ain't got to leave if you ain't never left!"

"Watch your mouth!" Whipping her neck and rolling her eyes, she just smirks. Lord knows that child got the devil in her, always has. The more that I look at her, the worse off I feel.

"Yeah, whatever."

Coming face to face with her now, I'm quick to stand my ground. "Bridgett, sit down." Hearing the seriousness in my voice, she flops down like that's the last thing that she wants to do. Humph.. . . .yeah, I still got it. Turning to Tammie now, "Tammie, go to your room."

Sorry that she's going to miss all of the action, she sits up trying her best to protest the issue. "But Momma Dee, I didn't even get my breakfast yet—"

"And you won't get it if you don't leave this instance." With that she storms off, leaving me and Bridgett alone at the table. Taking my seat, I'm face-to-face with my mini me. "Ok Bridgett, what's going on?"

"Nothing."

"Bridgee come on, this is Momma that you're talking to. Coming in here yelling and fussing like you've lost every good bone in your body. Oh yes, something's wrong. Child, don't you know that I carried you for 9 months, sat in labor 17 hours, washed you up and cared for you from the moment you stepped foot on this Earth up until now. Now I don't care how you treat this person or that, but in my house, you WILL respect me—"

"What you forgot? You didn't raise me, Grandma did! She raised all of us, because you were too busy going in and out of the streets, jumping from one man's bed to the next, remember? And you think just because you clean yourself up and go to church every now and then that that makes everything ok..." stunned and shocked, I just stare at her. My Lord, she just doesn't understand does she? Watching her get up from the table, she continues on and helplessly, I just watch. "... Well it doesn't! Sonya and Lamar can stay around here if they want to and act like you're some Saint, but I'm not!" watching her grab her coat and purse, my heart feels for her. With tears rolling down my face, I get up and go after her.

"Is that really what you think? I was only 16 when I had Sonya. And the years that followed, honey I was just trying to catch up on life, not knowing that I was missing yours. . ." walking a few steps closer to her. "Now I know that I wasn't perfect, but I've always. . . .always tried to do what was best for ya'll—"

"What was best for us? No momma, you mean what was best for you!" walking toward the door, she turns back for a moment. "I'm out of here. I'll see ya'll later."

"Where are you going?"

"Far away from you!"

Following her to the gate, "Bridgett! . . . Bridgett!" but just like that, she's gone. . . into the streets, yet again. Seeing her walk away, she reminds me every bit of myself. Oh how I must've hurt my mother. Oh my poor Bridgee, ...Lord, she just doesn't understand. Coming back toward the house, I stop on the porch just to cry my own lonely tears. Taking a seat on the step, I look out with no one to comfort me but momma's rose bushes. Oh good Lord, they always seem to bloom brightest at times like this. Looking at them now, it's almost like they're opening up their petals to the sound of my tears. Grabbing the closest one, even with the thorns I hold it as tight as I can. It's like momma always said, *'Sometimes, it's easier to stick your neck out for a rose rather than a person, because at least the rose will love you back.'*

Heading inside now, I look up toward the hills in which my Lord sits, and I cry out with the only plea left on the inside of me. "Lord, help me!"

Closing the door behind me, I'm surprised to find someone waiting for me.

"Momma Dee, you ok?" seeing Zectric stare at me with such expectancy, I quickly wipe away my tears and adorn my face with a smile. A mother's job is never over.

"Oh baby, I just had something in my eye that's all honey. That's all."

"Was that Auntie that just left?" My Jesus, how long has he been standing there? Unable to lie this time, I decide to face the truth in a sly sort of way.

"My, my, nothing gets past this 7 year old now does it?" Smiling that big old grin of his, he proudly admits to it with a nod of his head. "Well, seems to me that a young man thinking like that should get some breakfast quick, fast, and in a hurry. What do you think?" shaking his head, he leaps toward the table like it's his birthday or something.

"Sounds good to me. What are you cooking?"

"Oh, just some grits, eggs, scary bacon, and monster biscuits for my growing boy." Passing a plate his way.

After taking a bite, he replies with a mouth full of food. "Momma Dee's Famous!"

"Yeah,. . . ." sitting to the table with a plate of my own now. "It's my famous alright!" with us both laughing, my mind falls back to my own children. I want so much for them, but it seems almost like they're never going to get it. . . . Nope, not until it's time for them to fill my shoes. Good Lord, with the way that things are going, I pray that that ain't no time soon. . . no time soon.

***

April 29, 2015

Tammie

I didn't think that I would make it, but Lord, look at me. I'm standing here today to receive the top Math Student award for the past 9weeks. I have on my Sunday's best standing beside those up and coming, with my brand new outfit, I look better than new money. Looking into the stands, Momma Dee's smile is the only face that I want to see. She doesn't know that I'm getting an award today, so I'm excited just thinking about the look on her face. She'll be happy and more than proud of me. I did it momma! I did it!

Looking into the stands, boy these seats sure are filling up fast. I hope that momma gets here quick so that I won't have to—

"Hey, little lady!" scared out of my mind, I whip around to see who just crept up behind me. Catching my breath, good Lord, it's only Lamar. Stumbling in here, smelling like a smoke steel with a hint of alcohol.

"What are you doing here?"

"What do you mean 'what am I doing here'? I'm here to see you."

Sort of embarrassed by the way he's looking and staggering (talking all loud like nobody can hear him), I just look down and press my skirt. Good grief Momma Dee, where are you? Sucking up my courage, "Oh, well you didn't have to, because Momma Dee's—"

Putting a finger over my mouth and shaking his head like he's twice remedial, he manages to get out a few words. "No, . . . nope. . . .Momma told me. . . . ." Pointing to himself as if there's somebody else to choose from. ". . . me. . . to come out today."

"Well really, you don't have to, because she's coming—"

"Nope, she ain't coming."

Taken aback for a moment, "Well, why not? Momma Dee never misses my—"

"I don't know. All I know is that she told me to come here, and I'm here. . . . So, that's that." Watching him stumble his way to the bleachers, boy I can tell what kind of disaster that this is going to be.

Chapter 2:
May 10, 2015

Bridgett

"Hey, where are you going?" breathes Gerald, rolling over half a sleep.

"To the bathroom. I'll be back."

"Alright, don't go too far." Kissing him on the cheek as I roll from underneath him. Oh my God, he feels like a ton of steel. Looking at him as I stand up, he can stand to lose a few pounds that's for sure.

Going to the living room, I slouch on the couch and turn on the TV. I tell you after 2am, you really can't find anything worth watching on TV. Feeling disappointed, I cut the TV off and resort to my own thoughts.

I'll be glad when tomorrow comes. Gerald will leave around 9 or so to go see his wife, which makes me no never mind. She can have him and the kids, and I'll keep what I got right here. Please believe me, four days of him is enough for me. All this: 'I'm hungry, can you fix me something to eat,' 'I miss you, what time are you coming home,' 'I'm thirsty, can you grab me a beer,' is getting slap on my nerves. Lord knows that man is driving me up the wall! I keep telling that fool, I am not wifey. I'm not going to cook, clean, wait up with him, and sleep with him every time he rolls over just because he decided to grace me with his presence. Oh no, that ain't me. He knew when he got with me that I refuse to be tied down by anybody, and no, he will not change that.

Rolling over on the couch, I continue on. I have to remember to get some money from him before he leaves tomorrow too, or else we're going to be behind on rent again this month. And Mrs. Walker don't be playing about that rent money. She'll put you out quick.

But back to Gerald, do you know that that man had the nerve to ask me 'when were we going to start trying for a baby?' Boy please! He already has three kids of his own with his wife. Shoot, I'm not trying to be pregnant and barefoot, another Sonya in the making. Oh no! Ain't no babies coming here.

Buzz! Buzz!

Hearing my phone vibrate, I'm careful to see who it is. Folks don't call you at this time of night unless they want something.

Buzz! Buzz!

Looking at the number, it looks to be the house phone at Momma's. Oh Lord, what does she want now! Not really wanting to pick it up, I do anyway just in case it's important, which it probably isn't. "Hello."

"Auntie, that you?"

"Who is this?" sitting up now.

"Zectric." Lord that's Sonya's boy. What in the world is he doing up?

"Boy, what do you want? And why aren't you in bed?"

"Do you know how to wake Momma Dee up?"

"What? Boy, bye." Lord, I know that that child ain't call me for no foolishness like this. "Why would you ask me something like that?"

"I don't know. I tried to wake her up, but she's not waking up. She told me to get her up around 1:30am, so she'll make her shift at 3am. But she's still sleep."

"Did you shake her?"

"I did."

"Look Zectric, as much as I would love to help you right now. I'm kind of sleep. So just go get your momma or your uncle Lamar and tell them to wake her up."

"I can't. Momma and Uncle Lamar went out." Well that figures, those two ain't never been much for homebodies. And momma has the nerve to jump on my case. At least I'm not leaching off of her like the rest of 'em.

"Well, go get Tammie."

"I can't, Tammie left. She went to go visit her friend."

"Wait a minute, it's 2 am and Momma let Tammie leave?"

"No, Tammie went through her window, and she told me not to tell." Well, she messed up on that one. Good grief, that child ain't even 13 years old, and she's already sneaking out. Momma's got something on her hands with that one.

"Well, ... I guess the secrets out then, huh?" laughing a little to myself. "Look kid, Momma's probably just super tired. She works a lot, you know. So just give her a few minutes and try it again alright?"

"But Auntie, I'm hungry. Momma Dee always fixes me a mid-night snack before she goes to work."

"Well, fix it yourself." Fully irritated at the moment.

"I can't." sounding just as babyish as ever, I promise you, Momma Dee has that boy straight spoiled rotten.

"Why not?"

"Momma Dee told me not to go in the kitchen without an adult." Shifting myself in the chair.

"Ok boy, just give me a minute, alright. I'll be right there."

"Ok."

"Oh and Zectric, how did you get my number."

"Momma Dee put it on speed dial and told me to press one in case of emergencies."

Laughing a little to myself now. "And I guess this was an emergency?"

"Yep, Momma Dee said that if she was late for work again, she wouldn't get paid as much. So she made me promise to wake her up."

"Well,. . . . she told the right one. I'll see you in a minute, ok."

"Ok, but you have to hurry, because Momma Dee's going to be late for work if you don't."

"Ok." Hanging up the phone, I sit up and prepare myself for what looks to be a sleepless night. Well, up we go!

Chapter 3:
May 10, 2015

Momma Dee

Sitting here thinking how peaceful it must be to have no worries, no burdens, and Lord knows no stressors. Feeling this good, I almost don't want to get up. Looking around now, I see myself, lying on the bed not moving a muscle. Sleep on Momma Dee... Sleep On.

Seeing Zectric and Bridgee shake me back and forth, it's almost like their worried or something. But not me,... I feel alright. Watching helplessly as Bridgee falls to her knees and Zectric runs out, it's clear to me that something must be wrong. But still, I sleep on.... I sleep on.

Oh poor Bridgee, she looks sad enough. But I'm ok,...I'm ok.

Looking now away from the bed and into my hands, I'm carrying a little basket with little roses inside. Oh how this brings back so many memories! Every year, momma used to have me tending to that rose garden of hers, but to tell you the truth, I kind of hated it. All of those rose bushes had thorns on 'em. I pricked my hand every time I'd pick one. But momma would just smile and tell me *'You can't have 'em bloom without the thorns, because all good things come from pain.'* Oh momma!

Picking up the roses now, it's like the petals are crying. Each wet tear falling one at a time. Looking back at the bed now, my poor Bridgee is holding me now, trying her best to breathe life back into me. Ah baby, you can't revive what the Lord has already called home. The more she tries, the harder that the roses cry. So I put the roses back in the basket, and turn around and walk away. Away, away. . . .far away. I don't know where I'm going, but I'm going anyway. Poor Bridgee, if only you knew how awful it feels to stand in my shoes. Poor Bridgee, I'll be praying for you. Poor Bridgee, this is just something that you'll just have to do. . . .my poor Bridgee. With no other way to vent, I sing. I sing the only song that's still in my heart. Singing to the beat, pitter-pat . . . . pitter-pat:

"At the gate I know, at the gate I know, at the gate I know, somebody's waiting at the gate I know. My mother, she'll be waiting at the gate I know. My mother, she'll be waiting at the gate I know. My mother will be waiting for me at the gate I know."

***

Lamar

Man do I enjoy nights like this. No worries, no bills,. . . . just a few drinks, table full of friends, and much needed laughter; and considering the week that I've had, this almost seems too good to be true. Down here at Charley's, you've got everything, from shooting pole, card games, dancing, constant flow of people, and who could forget the entertainment. Tonight's comedy night, so a bunch of local comedians team up to get their funny on. In a big city like this, people always trying to be the next big thing. The guy on stage right now is every bit of a loser, but drunk as I am right now, I'm not going to be the one to tell him.

"Come on Lamar, are you going to post up on that chair all night?" rushing to the table for the umpteenth time, Sonya seems to be exhausted. But when you've been caged with a no good man for about 2/3 years, I guess that'll do it to you.

"Nah, not me. . . ." as I pause to take a sip of my drink. ". . .Dancing ain't for me. Besides, you seem to be doing alright by yourself. I'll just sit here and watch the drinks." And just like that, there she goes back on the dance floor hunting for husband #3. I already told her, with two kids and already twice divorced, maybe marriage just ain't her thing. I mean, she already struck out two times, there's no need to go for a third one. As I take another look at this place, it's like everybody's here running from something, whether it be relationships, family, bills, job, or etc. Everybody's running from something, and the reason that I know this to be true is because who in their right mind would stay out partying 'til 3am in the morning if they had something to look forward to? My point exactly. Everybody's here for a reason, but as for me, I'm just tired of it all you know. It's like I hate going home, but I don't have any other place to go. From the time I walk in up until the time that I leave, Momma's always on my case about something: whether it be about getting a job, helping out with the bills, or even settling down with somebody. That's all in my ear, 24/7. And you know the crazy part about it, she's sweating me about stuff that she ain't even do! I watched momma when she was my age. She couldn't keep a job, couldn't hold a man, and she sure couldn't contribute to any bills. I don't know how many eviction notices that I've seen. Man if it wasn't for grandma, there'd be many nights that we would've slept on the streets. Momma was just like Sonya and Bridgett growing up, so she doesn't have any room to fuss at anybody. Shoot, according to grandma (God bless the dead), she slept with her own stepdad to get me. Now, she goes around places talking that church talk like she's perfect or something. But for the sake of argument, I just keep my mouth closed, 'cause every bad wind can change. Shoot, ain't that what the good book say?

Ring! Ring!

As I look at my phone, it's Momma. Speak of the devil!

Ring! Ring!

Man, I really don't want to pick this up. All she wants to do is nag me about hanging out for the third time this week. But staying with her, I got to go out to keep myself sane!

Ring! Ring!

Half-heartedly giving in, I pick up the phone. "Hello."

"Lamar! . . . Lamar!. . . ." it's Zectric yelling through the receiver in between sobs. "Come quick! . . . You've got to hurry and—"

Feeling the conversation to be more serious now, I put my drink down and sit up. "Just calm down, calm down, and tell me what happened."

"It's Momma Dee. . . she's. . . she's-"

"Momma? What's wrong with her? Is she alright?"

"No, . . . no. . . .I tried to wake her, but she. . . she. . . she won't wake up. Uncle Lamar, she won't wake up! . . . .she just. . . she won't. . . .she-"

"Zectric, sweetie give me the phone." Hearing Bridgett in the background, I get up from my chair. If he called Bridgett, things have to be bad. "Hello, Lamar is that you?"

"Yeah, yeah. . .it's me. What's going on? Tell me what it is."

"It's momma. . ." as the silence follows, I can hear Bridgett crying her own tears. Hearing the sorrow in her voice, my tears start to flow, one after another. Each one faster than the last. "She's. . . .oh God!. . . Momma's dead. She's gone. . .Momma's gone-"

Hearing the words from the other end, my whole body goes numb, and as my fingers rest, the phone falls, . . . leaving me standing, too paralyzed to move. My soul on the inside of me screams tearful pleas, but my lips say nothing. Oh momma. . . oh momma, why did you leave me? Why did you leave?

"Hey, what's up? Are you alright?" looking around, it's Sonya. Caught up in my own feelings, I didn't even notice her come up, but the tears in my eyes must've frightened her.

Taking a step back, I've got nothing to hide and no room to run, not anymore. I just lay it all on the line, as real as it can get. "We have to go home. Momma's dead."

Hearing her gasp, I reach out to catch her before she falls. In a room full of people, no one sees our pain, and no one hears our cries, but everyone's still laughing, still drinking, still living. . .

Chapter 4:
May 21, 2015

Bridgett

"Good grief, are you done already?" turning back, it's only Zectric. No surprise there. "You've had to have been cleaning that same spot for about an hour now."

Smiling half-way to myself, I hate to admit it, but he's right. I've been running myself crazy cleaning this kitchen to pieces, but not even the smell of bleach can help me now. Gripping the clothe in my hand, I return the cleaner back to its rightful place. Meanwhile, I'm still trying to find mine. Taking my seat at the table, it's just him, me, and those God awful roses sitting in the middle of the table.

"Looks like it's time to change the roses." That Zectric I tell you, he has all of the answers today, but sadly he's right. Looking at them now, the petals are browning as if they're sad too. But I've never been much for messing with roses, that's always been momma's thing. Every so often, momma would pick new ones to go into the vase, but I could never get into it. Those thorns hurt way too much for me to be picking them, so I haven't.

"Yeah, it looks that way doesn't."

"Sooooo, are you going to change them?"

"Oh no, roses, I don't really get into them like that. They're not really my thing."

Looking at me like my very reply crushes his hope, he manages to muffle his reply. "They were Momma Dee's thing." Locking eyes with him, my eyes fill up. What was he expecting? I'm not, ...I can never be. . . . .momma. No one can!

With tears rolling down my cheeks, I break eye contact with him. I couldn't look into his eyes right now, because my heart has nothing to say. Not right now. "Yeah, . . . yeah, it was." Laughing half-heartedly to myself, momma's been gone for a little over a week, but the pain's still just as real as the night that we found her. . . ice cold and motionless. She looked so calm, like she was finally . . . finally at peace.

"So, ...what's for breakfast?" catching me in the midst of my thoughts, I'm boom-fondled. Wait, what?

"Breakfast?"

"Yeah, you know it's what normal people eat in the morning." Sarcastically as he knows how.

"Yeah big-head, I know what it is."

"Then where is it?"

Getting up from the table, I manage to pull out some Fruit Loops from the cabinet. Well, that's breakfast then. But as I place them in front of him, his crystal stare tells me that I'm wrong yet again.

"Really? I don't eat Fruit Loops, Tyrell does. Momma Dee would never give me that."

"Well why not?"

"I'm lactose intolerant."

Picking the cereal up, looking just as lost as ever. "Well, can't you eat it dry?"

"Are you serious? Where's the grits, eggs, and toast?" Good God, I know that momma wasn't cooking for this boy every day. There's no way that I can follow that up, and besides, this boy *has* a mother. Speaking of which, where is she?

"Well, you know what. When Sonya gets here, she can fix you—"

"Sonya's not here."

Wait a minute, don't tell me that he and Sonya are on a first name bases. No wonder why momma took him under her wing. "Well where is she smartie?"

"She's at Randy's house, they're supposed to be getting married soon."

"Well, why didn't she take you and Tyrell?"

Shrugging his shoulders, he just turns and says, "He's not too big on kids, so we stay with Momma Dee." Wait, what? Are you kidding me? Sonya just dumps her kids off like that. Well she and I are going to have to talk pretty soon, because I'm not momma. Shoot, I'm only 21 and I've got a life of my own.

"Well, I didn't know that."

"You wouldn't." turning to Tammie who's just walked in. She sits at the table grabbing the cereal, and eats it straight out of the box. Really? Who in the world does this child thinks she is?

"And what's that supposed to mean?"

"It means you don't know what you're doing here! And to be honest I don't either." Looking at her rolling her eyes and popping her neck just as sassy as ever. Who in the world is this child playing with? Because it ain't me.

"Wait little lady, I'm the older one ok. That means you do what I say."

"Since when?"

"Since right now. Talking like you ain't got no sense. But since you're here,. . ." sitting down in the chair next to her. "Where were you last night?"

"Huh? I was in my bed—"

"Girl who do you think that you're fooling? You leave out your bed three or four times a week and get in two hours before you have to get up in the morning like nobody knows."

Turning her eyes from me to Zectric, "Snitch! I should've known that you couldn't keep your mouth shut."

"I didn't say anything." Trying desperately to plead his case.

"He didn't have to tell me." Catching her attention again. Looking at me with that deer in the headlights blank stare, my God she's something ain't she. "I was your age before remember? And I can tell you from experience, there's nothing out at that time of night for a 12 year old."

"13."

"And when was this? You're birthday ain't here yet."

"Well, I'm almost—"

"Almost grounded if you keep it up."

"You can't tell me what to do?" standing up from the table and yelling like she's hot and bothered all of a sudden. Good Lord, these kids today. This is the perfect reason why I don't have kids of my own.

"Why not?" standing face to face with her now.

"Because you're not my mother! My mother's dead." with us both feeling the sting of her words, it's hard to come back from that. So not really knowing what to do, I sit back down and watch helplessly as Tammie breaks down for the first time. Seeing her cry, I want so bad to reach her, but I know that I can't. She took momma's death pretty hard. She wouldn't even come to the funeral. Oh momma, what in the world have I gotten myself into.

"What's going on here?" looking up the stairwell, it's Lamar. Leave it to him to come when the hard parts over. Getting myself together, I stand up and grab Zectric's and Tyrell's things.

"Just getting ready for school. Are you heading out?"

"Yeah for a little bit."

"Good, then you can take Tammie and the boys to then school then, right?" looking him dead in his eyes, it's clear to me that that's not really what he had in mind.

"Nah, I got this thing to do in a few, and –"

"A thing? You don't have a job. What THING can you possibly have that can stop you from taking ten minutes out of your day to drop them off at school?"

Rolling his eyes and frowning his face, my Lord does everyone have an attitude this morning? Am I the only one that woke up on the right side of the bed? "Man sis, don't start."

"Start what? Telling you the truth. I've gotten all the kids up, clothed them, feed them—" seeing Zectric cut his eyes up at me, I quickly realize that I have to take that comment back. "Well, I tried to feed them, but my point is, Momma's not here anymore. The least that you and Sonya can do is help me out. I mean come on, I'm the only one working in the house, and I have to do all of this too?"

"Man, I'm gone. You're starting to sound just like momma." Slamming the screen door behind him, he yells back, "And don't wait up for me either. I'll be back when I'm back."

Going to the door now, I watch as Lamar jumps into the car with a few of his friends, leaving me here . . . .alone. . . .again. Oh momma, I really need you to help me on this one. Slowly turning back, I now see three faces staring back at me,. . . all of them expecting me to be. . . . the one and only Momma

Dee. Well, it doesn't look like that's going to happen anytime soon.

"Well, come on ya'll. If we don't hurry, all of you will be late for school." And with that, the four of us head out . . .oh momma, what am I to do now?

***

Tammie

There's a scripture (Psalms 30:5) that reads, 'Weeping may endure for a night, but joy comes in the morning.' As I sit here at the table it feels like the nights just seem to be getting longer and longer with each day that passes. I miss you so much. Nobody's getting along. Everything is falling apart. And most nights, all I want to do is touch you or even see you. God could've taken anyone, but why did it have to be you? We need you momma, ...I need you. . . .

"Tammie! . . . Hello?" caught up in the moment I look up. Oh, it's only Breyah, my best friend since before I can remember. "Girl, are you in space or something? 'Cause we only have a few more minutes before lunch is over, and you haven't even touched your food."

"Oh, I'm not really hungry." Sitting up now preparing myself for the long drown out conversation that I know is coming. I love Breyah, but Lord knows that child can talk. Looking around the lunchroom, everybody's laughing and enjoying themselves, probably because school's about to let out in a few days.

"Really? Girl, I've known you forever and a day and I've never heard you say anything like that." Eyeing me for a moment. "Ah no, don't tell me you still hanging on to that what's-his-face?"

"What?" now she's really lost me.

"Please, don't act like you don't know who I'm talking about. Brandon that's who. Does that name ring a bell?"

"Oh gosh no."

"Then why are you staring at him. He's way across the room." Looking back at her, she's right. He is across the room, but I've been so caught up in my own thoughts that I didn't even notice that I was looking in his direction. Kind of embarrassed, I quickly turn away.

"Man please, I'm not even thinking about him?"

"Good, because with them hand-me-downs on, he won't even talk to you." Looking down at my wardrobe, she's right. I sure wouldn't want him to see me like this. With wrinkled jeans, a plaid shirt, and sneakers, I'm not even semi-cute today. Note to self, don't let Bridgett pick out your clothes anymore. That's one thing that I do miss about momma, after picking out our clothes and ironing them, we always looked A-1 leaving the house. "I mean, I know that it's spring and all, but for real just pick a color. You don't have to come to school wearing the whole rainbow." Catching me off guard, I can't help but laugh. Leave it to Breyah to make me smile on a cloudy day. I guess that's why we're friends.

"Yeah whatever. . . .Anyway, did you bring it for me?"

"Girl what do I look like? Pic-N-Save?"

"Come on, lunch is almost over. Do you have it or not?" with only a few more minutes left, I have to do this thing now or never, because once we go to third period, I won't even see her until we get on the bus.

Removing a brown paper bag from her backpack, she slowly hands it to me. "Wait a minute!" snatching the bag back at the last minute like it's somebody's ransom or something. "Why do you need this anyway? I mean, it's not like you need it."

Oh good Lord, I promise you that she's the nosiest person I know. Still with the clock ticking, I have to tell her something. Getting up from the table, I throw my book bag on my back. "Girl, come on.."

"Why? Where are you going?"

Really? Does she have to do this now? "To the bathroom."

"Oh no, I don't have to go." Frustrated to the max, I grab her by the arm and drag her with me anyway. Really not wanting to be late for class, as soon as we make it to the hallway, I take off for the bathroom which is on the opposite end of the hall. Not wanting to get left behind, Breyah picks up the pace as well.

Reaching the bathroom, I push the door open and quickly check each and every stall. I really don't want to tell Breyah anything. But if I have to, I'm definitely going to make sure that nobody else hears it. People around here are good for ease dropping.

Now that the coast is clear, it's just me and Breyah. And judging by the look on her face, she demands an explanation. Taking a deep breath, I finally gather the courage to give her one. "Ok, it's like this. I went out for a few nights to hang out with Brandon—"

"Yeah, I remember you told that already. But girl how did you pull that off, you know Momma Dee had you on that strict curfew. Shoot, you couldn't even watch TV that late."

"I know." Leaning back, I hold the sink as tight as I can. "I may have snuck out a few times."

"Girl, no!!!!"

"It was only because I knew that momma would never let me go."

"So you went anyway? Girl, you are so bad!"

"Yeah. . . .I sort of. . . did." Shrugging my shoulders from shame. It's crazy, Momma Dee is dead and gone and I still feel guilty.

"Girl don't stop there, tell me. Tell me everything." With a smile so wide and her eyes so big, you would have thought that I was on Saturday Night Live or something. Good God, she loves to be in somebody else's business. But knowing that she has something that I need, I go on and tell her all that she wants to hear.

"You see, I went to Tim's house for the party, and. . . . well, I tried to talk to Brandon. You know,. . .. to get his attention, but he was all over Monica. . . ." turning to look at myself in the mirror. Looking myself up and down, nothing looks too appealing from here. I'm just as plain-jane as a girl can get. Maybe if I wore some lipstick or even make-up, I'd be prettier. Look at me, my eyes are too round, my cheeks are too fat, and my hair is way too thick. I can't do anything with it, and momma would never let me put any weave in it. All she ever did was put it in a ponytail with ribbons. How many times do I have to tell her? I'm not three. I'm 13, ...well almost. "He didn't even notice me."

"Well girl it's his lost. And Monica? Really? That girl is a real piece of work. She walks around here like she's America's Next Top Model or something."

"Yeah she does." Turning to her in agreement.

Ding! Ding!

"Well, that's the bell. Girl, I'll see you—"

Trying my best to stop her, I grab her arm. "Breyah, I think that I'm pregnant."

Looking at me in shock, she turns back to me. "For who? Brandon?"

"No, not him. You see—"

"How? Wait, when did this happen?"

"Well, I went to see Brandon, but he could've cared less. So I was kind of stuck there with no one to talk to, and I ran into T.J.—"

"Wait, T.J? Ill, that man is grown. He's like almost 30."

"24."

"Ain't he friends with your brother Lamar? Ain't he the one that be coming over to ya'll house all of the time? Really---"

"Yeah, well he was there—"

"Why? I thought that that was a teenage party."

"It was people there of all ages. It was like a block party or something. I guess Tim just likes to have get-together's every now and then."

"Girl whatever. Just finish the story."

"Well, . . . I went to a couple of the parties, and he was always there. And one night, he offered me a ride home, but. . . .we didn't go straight home. . . Come to think of it, we didn't go straight home a few times. . ." leaning back, I brace the sink yet again, because in the state that I'm in, it's the only thing sturdy enough to hold me up. "He started out just touching me. . . .then he started kissing on me. . . .And I wanted him to stop, I did, but. . . . .it just felt good, you know. . ." cutting my eyes back at the reflection behind me, all I can see is a girl crying tears for me. Ashamed of her in her weakness, I put my head back down. "It felt good to be held,. . .to be told that I was pretty. . . even beautiful at times. . ." with each passing word, my heart begins to sink further and further down. Almost like gravity's got its hold on it, pulling it harder and harder. And I begin to feel all of the pain at once. Not really wanting to be this emotional, I try my best to change the subject. Not for me, but for the nameless reflection standing behind me. The lost girl who struggles to be seen. The lost, nameless girl that just happens to be me. "I've been feeling pretty bad for a few weeks. The week of momma's funeral, I was so out of it that I didn't even go. All this pain, nausea, and vomiting, ...I feel like I can just throw up at the site of food sometimes. Not to mention the fact that I haven't seen any sign of my period in over a month." Turning back to her now. "Girl, I really. . .really need that test."

Taking a minute, she stares at me as if to search my eyes for the truth or lies. Not sure of what to make of it herself, she grabs the brown paper bag from her backpack and hands it to me. "Girl just take it. Take it."

Taking the bag, I go into the nearest stall. As the seconds turn into minutes, I sit aimlessly while Breyah paces the floor back and forth. While we wait, I hear a few knocks, but Breyah's a true friend. She wouldn't dare let anyone else in.

The test itself really didn't take that long, but I just couldn't look at it right away. What if I was pregnant? I'm only 12 years old. What am I going to do with a baby? And then again, what if I wasn't? I just told my only secret to the biggest Mouth-of-the-South. I love Breyah to death, but God knows she can't hold water. Taking a deep breath, I flip the stick over. Sure enough, I'm pregnant. Staring at the stick, I can't even believe my eyes. Losing it, I hit the stick against the bathroom stall trying my best to get the screen to change. But with every blow. . . . .it held its ground. Hearing all of the commotion, Breyah comes to the stall.

"Girl are you ok? Open the door. Girl open the door." Unlocking the door, I look up at her. With tears in my eyes, I manage to say the words that I, myself, didn't even want to hear.

"I'm pregnant." In total disbelief, Breyah takes both the stick and the box from me.

"Girl no, you must've read it wrong or something." Scanning the box and the stick both, she too concludes what I already know to be true. "Yeah. . . .you're pregnant."

Oh momma, I need you right now. Oh momma. . .help me. . . please.

***

Momma Dee

Looking down at my baby, I so badly want to say, '*I hear you sweet baby. I hear you.*' Lord knows I want to be there for her. But there are some things in life that we are made to face alone. My baby, ...my poor baby. . . .

Looking down at my hands, I'm still holding the basket with roses. I guess momma was right. They do bloom best at times like these. Picking up a rose, oh such a pretty rose, I watch as the petals begin to fall, one by one. Holding the rose as tight as I can, the petals yet and still fall like little tears from a desperate man.

I guess it's true, roses can cry just like me and you. Before turning to leave, I carefully place the rose on the ground, allowing it to cry once more. When the last leaf falls, all that is left is the stem. Being bare and naked, I stand it up in the ground. Just like the rose that is still able to stand, so will Tammie be, all she has to do is to hold onto God's unchanging hand.

Looking at her now, I simply just shake my head and leave with these words, '*My child, my child, I see you. You'll have to raise a baby even though you're a child too. Don't get lost in grief and please dry your weeping eyes. I know that it's hard, but if I had to do it, so do you.*'

Chapter 5:
Bridgett

"What? Ok, I'll be right there." Hanging up the phone, I jump out of the bed and do my best to find my clothes.

"Who's that baby?" asks Gerald as he raises his head from underneath the covers.

"Nobody, just some lady from the school."

"Oh, that sounds serious." frowning at me sarcastically.

"Shut-up!" as I lean over to kiss him, he's just smiling at me. "What?"

"I don't know. I've never seen you like this."

"Like what?"

"Like this, all motherly and everything. 'Oh you have to go to the school.'" With us both laughing now, I have to admit whether I want to or not, I am taking on a new role. . . one that I never wanted, and still don't.

"Yeah, I guess you're right." Sitting up now, I go back to putting on my clothes. "But if I don't, who is? Lamar's still hanging out like he's 16, and Sonya can't stay put for five seconds."

"Then just leave." Turning to look at him, it's clear that he's serious. Even though he stole the words from my heart, it's the way that he's saying it. Like. . . .like it's that easy. Is it?

"Really?"

"Yeah, you don't need them. You've got me." Getting up from the bed now, like Captain Saver he comes to rescue me from the life that I never wanted. The more I kiss him and the more he touches me, the freer I feel. I'm no mom, and I've got my own life to live.

Standing here with him almost makes me forget about Tammie completely. Today was my day off, the last thing that I want to do is to spend it at some school. Knowing her, whatever the case, it was probably her fault. That child's always been stubborn. The lady from the school told me that it's urgent that I get there. Really? Unless she burned down the school, how urgent can it be?

"See baby, you don't need them. You've got me." Looking up at me now.

"Yeah well, I'll see you when I get back."

"All man! Now what am I supposed to do while you're gone?"

"Ummm, let's see. Call your wife and tell her that she's been replaced for the week. And tell the kids that you'll see them later." With us both laughing now, seemingly to be a joke, it'd be nice if that were true.

"Well that could work, let's see. . . we could go to Destin, rent a room, and have us a nice time. There's just one catch to that."

"What?"

"You have to leave that Huddle job behind." Laughing again, leave it to Gerald to make me smile. And with the last few weeks that I've had, I need it. "Call in sick or something?"

"Yeah, yeah." Backing up to the door now. "I'll see you when I get back." Closing the door behind me.

Driving to the school house now, reality quickly takes the wheel. What in the world is wrong with that child? I know that she's the baby and all, but Zectric and Tyrell don't even act like this. Maybe it's like Gerald said, I'm getting way too caught up in this. I mean, when momma passed, I tried to help out around the house just to be nice and everything. But at the end of the day, shoot I got a life too.

Reaching the school, I don't have to walk far. The principal's office is right by the front door. Walking into the office, it's like there's this deep sense of dread that somehow just covers the room. With Tammie and the Principal both locking their eyes on me, I anxiously take my seat.

"Hello ma'am. My name is Principal Smith." Extending her hand across the table, I shake her hand. "How are you?"

"I'm fine."

"And you are?"

"Oh, I'm Bridgett, Tammie's sister." Looking around the room, it's like nobody wants to start the meeting. Getting highly impatient, I decide to start the conversation. "So uh, what's going on?"

"First off, I want to start by saying that I'm sorry for your lost, and I hate touching bases with you on these terms. But we just had a situation occur today, and I felt the need to reach out to some of Tammie's closest relatives."

"What? And I'm the closest?"

"Well ma'am looking at her file, there are only three relatives listed." Putting her glasses on, she looks down at the file on her desk. Good Lord, what did Tammie do? Everybody knows that if somebody has to pull your file, you've really done something. "There's a Ms. Sonya Wright, a Mr. Lamar Taydum, and yourself, a Ms. Bridgett Rogers." Looking back up at me, she puts the file back in its rightful place. "I called Mrs. Sonya, but I didn't get an answer. I called Mr. Lamar, but the number was not active. You were the only person that was able to be reached."

"Ok."

"Well, after lunch, we had a bathroom incident. Tammie and another student locked themselves in the restroom, and refused to open it. We had to get a janitor to unlock the doors. And when we did, . . . " picking up a brown bag from her drawer, she shoves it my way. "We found this." Opening the bag, I'm floored by what I see.

"What's this?" turning my attention to Tammie now. Looking up at me with tears in her eyes, she struggles to speak. "Tammie what is it?"

"It's a pregnancy test."

Holding up the stick now, "It's got a plus on it. What does this mean Tammie?" unable to pull herself together, she puts her head down and cries even harder this time. Turning back to the principal now. "Well, didn't you say that it was another student there today?"

"Yes ma'am it was."

"Then where is she? Why isn't she here?"

"Well, because Tammie admitted that it was her test."

"What?" turning back to Tammie now. "What?" not willing to answer me, she just cries. Good God, how stupid can this girl be? Momma ain't been gone but two weeks, and I've got to deal with all of this. She ain't legal. She ain't nothing but 12. My Lord, my Lord.

Completely frustrated at this point, I get up from my chair. "Get up and come on." Grabbing Tammie by the arm in my anger, I turn back to the principal before leaving. "Thank you so much. She'll be coming with me. Have a nice day." So caught up in the moment, I didn't even pause to listen to the response. In three shakes of a minute, we are in the car and headed to the clinic. Enough with these home tests, I want to be sure. As I turn street corners and pass lights, it's like my whole world flashes before my eyes. Oh momma,. . . please help me. . . .

***

Lamar

"Man, you need to get you a ride?" turning to T.J. who's bent on complaining.

"Man shut-up. I got one, it just ain't fixed yet." Staring out of the window now with the windows down, because the gas needle is too low to run the AC, I get lost in my own thoughts. Man I can't believe Bridgett. I already told her that I had plans for today. Shoot, the boys and I were headed out for the weekend. But no, Bridgett just had to mess that up, telling me to pick up the boys. Man please, those are Sonya's kids. She needs to be getting them herself.

"Man, we've been sitting here for like an hour already. The boys aren't out of school yet?"

"That shows you how much you know. School kids don't get out until 3:15pm, and we ain't been here no hour. It's only been like thirty minutes. Leave it to you to choke something up."

"Why are we stuck out here anyway?"

"Something's up with Tammie. She had a doctor's appointment today, or so they say. But man, I told Bridgett a few days ago that that girl was sick. All that coughing and throwing up. . . shoot, ain't nobody grieving that hard."

"Shoot with all of that, I hope she's alright."

"Yeah, you and me both. . . .you and me both, 'cause I can't deal with them two bad boys of Sonya's. Both of them are bay-bay kids!"

"That's your kin."

"Yeah, whatever."

Ring! Ring!

Looking down at my phone, it's Bridgett, Ms. Want-To-Be-Momma. Not really wanting to answer it, I let it ring a few times.

Ring! Ring!

"Man, you better get that."

"Shut-up T.J. and mind your own business." Half-laughing to myself, I pick up the phone.

Listening to Bridgett on the other end, it's like the life is drained out of me. It's like I'm hearing the words, but not processing the meaning of them. Caught in this state, I ask her to repeat herself, and she does. With my heart jumping out of my chest, I turn to T.J. in complete shock.

"What's up man? You good?" he asks as he sits up in the seat now trying to pick my brain. But just thinking of how this man can even look at me with a straight face, just boils me.

"You've been messing with my sister?"

Sitting up and playing stupid, he tries to throw me for a loop. "Man, what are you talking about—"

But before he can even get the words out of his mouth, I go in for the kill. Two quick jabs to the left followed up by a right hook. The fight only lasts a few minutes, but it feels like hours. Pulled from the car by a school officer, we're taken downtown and booked for charges.

***

Momma Dee

Looking through the skies, I see my poor son ramping and raging, because life's no longer fun. Standing above him now, I feel his pain, and I hear his tears. '*My son, my son. . .*'

Pulling another rose from the basket still in my hand, the rose begins to cry its own tears. As the petals fall, my heart begins to ache. '*My dear son, I didn't raise you this way.*'

Before the last leaf falls, I stand the stem upright in the ground. '*My son, my son, . . .I guess the rose has cried all because you've finally figured out that smiling faces really do tell lies.. .*'

Chapter 6:
May 30, 2015

Bridgett

Lord have mercy on us today. Late for one evening and the school has had Sonya's two boys taken away. Leave it to Lamar to go on and get into a fight, the boys were left at the school without a ride. With Lamar in jail and the two boys in the state's care, I can't find rest anywhere. Sonya's gone nuts, it's like she doesn't even care. With the boys in a foster home, she's free to live life with no remorse in the air. Her and her new-boo have gone and eloped, while I'm trying to figure out how to pull this family together dead broke. It costs $550 to post Lamar's bail and another $1500 for Tammie's situation to go good-bye, farewell. Good Lord, don't they know that money doesn't grow on trees. It's like nothing is ever what it seems. . . .

Sitting at the table, those dying roses are still in the vase. If Zectric were here, he'd tell me to change them, but with him gone, that's just another thing that I can't do. Looking at them browned and withered, it's like their feeling the weight on my shoulders. They're crying out for me, saying the words that I can never speak. Realizing this, I hide my eyes and cry. Good Lord what do we do now? Momma has only been dead for a month, and everything. . . .and I mean everything. . . is falling apart.

Not really wanting to sit here in the midst of my emotions, I get up. I've got to get out of here; if I don't get out now, I never will. With Sonya and the boys gone, and Lamar in jail, nobody's here but me and Tammie. And we're far from getting along. Going upstairs, I see Tammie through her cracked door. She's fast asleep. Good, that means that I can get out without being seen. Going into my room, I grab everything that I can find: my clothes, my shoes, my toothbrush, . . .everything that can fit into my bags. Gerald was right. I can't be doing this. This is too much for anybody. While packing my clothes, I catch a glimpse of myself in the mirror. Who am I? And what am I doing? Seeing the girl in the mirror cry, my heart feels for her. She's so burdened and so weighted down. Her whole world has turned upside down. Seeing her face and feeling her pain, I can't take it. I can't take it anymore. . . So I do what I do best, I turn and head out of the door, leaving my bags and everything else behind. Running as fast as I can, I jet down the stairs and head straight for the door. One step and then two, I accidently trip over a shoe at the bottom of steps and tumble to the floor. Trying to catch myself, I end up bringing momma's stand down, emptying the drawer and its contents.

"Ooooh, God." Feeling my legs, nothing's broken, but with all of the pain, it may be a sprain.

"Hey, what's going on?" looking up, I see Tammie at the top of the stairs. Seeing me on the floor, she rushes to help me. "Oh God Bridgett, what happened?" as she tries to pull me up.

"Just help me up already, would you." Trying to stand up on my feet, it's clear that it's almost impossible. With the pain so vivid, there's no way that I'm making it to the chair, so Tammie pulls me to the nearest step.

"What were you doing?"

"I was coming down the steps and I tripped."

"Yeah, I can see that. Over what though?"

Pointing at the shoes on the floor, "Over momma's shoes."

Looking down at the shoes, Tammie just laughs. I'm so glad that she finds this so funny. "Why are you still keeping these shoes right there? Momma Dee's been gone for a minute now."

Feeling sort of embarrassed, I go ahead and fess up. "Momma always left her shoes there so that she could find them when she got ready to go to work. By keeping them there, it makes me feel like . . . .like this is all a dream. . . and she'll come back. It sounds crazy huh?"

Now looking at me with both love and care in her eyes, Tammie just smiles. "No. . . not to me."

Looking now at the mess on the floor, good grief it looks like I broke the stand. "I guess we have to pick that up." Looking down at the floor, Tammie just shakes her head. Trying my best to bend over, which is painful in itself, it's clear from my point of view that Tammie's going to be doing most of the picking up.

Still picking up the contents of the stand, which is mostly old mail, Tammie stands up and hands me a couple of letters. "What's this?"

Taking the letters, I sit on the step. Letter after letter I see the same thing, 'Important: Bill Enclosed,' 'Last Notice,' 'Final Correspondent,' and so on. Clueless, tears just seem to come to my eyes. Oh momma, why didn't you say anything?

"Well, what is it?"

Taking a deep breath, I tell her. "It looks like we're past due on property taxes, way overdue for loans, and three months behind on the mortgage, and these..." holding up the last two letters in my hand. "These are past due doctor bills. Look at the this." Showing her the last letters in my hand. "It looks as if momma was taking chemo treatments."

Reading the letter for herself, "But the death certificate said natural causes."

"I guess cancer *is* natural to some folks." As I sit on the step, my eyes drift downward to momma's fallen shoes. Oh momma, how awful it must have been to stand in your shoes. Being behind in bills, virtually about to lose the house, battling cancer, taking care of us, and working two jobs at the same time. Oh momma, . . . now I see your pain. . . .now I understand your heartache. . . . oh momma!

Sitting on the step, Tammie and I are both crying. With nowhere to run and nowhere to hide, we just sit and hug one another, each crying tears of the heart. Holding Tammie close, I vent the only way that I know how. The same way that momma used to. I sing. . . . the only song in my heart.

"God told Ezekiel. . . to go down in the valleeeeey. . . .of dry bones, dry bones. . . . Oh Lord, God tooooooold Ezekiel to go down in the valleeeey yeah, ...of dry bones, dry bones. . . . . and hear. . . oh hear the salvation of the Lord. . . ."

Crying tears in the midst of every verse, I now know the pain of the songwriter. Oh how awful it must feel to be led to the same dry places, the same dry situations, where things aren't getting any better no matter how hard you try. Oh the pain Ezekiel must have felt. No, ...the pain that I feel in *my* dry place. My finances are dry. I can't get money fast enough to take care all of this. My family is dry. Everything is falling apart, and I don't know what to do or where to go from here. Meanwhile, I'm so drained. I don't have anything else left to give.

Feeling the pain of my soul, I hold Tammie tighter and sing the song of a broken heart.

". . . God told me . . . . to go down, go down. . . . go in the valleeeeey of dry bones. . . . .dry, dry bones. . . .to hear the salvation of the Lord.. . . .yesssssssss, He did.. . ."

***

June 13, 2015

Bridgett

After the week that I've had, I need a night out, and from the looks of things, Tammie did too. Things still are kind of sour. I mean, I still haven't gotten the money to post

Lamar's bail, but T.J. did. Seems as how him and Lamar have been friends for so long, that was his way of making amends I guess. I'm not sure how Lamar is feeling about the situation, but I'm still pressing charges. My sister is less than five days away from her 13th birthday, there is no reason on God's green Earth why she should be carrying a baby. Especially for someone who's close to 30. Come to think of it, he's older than me. Some psycho.

Coming to my seat now carrying popcorn and drinks, I'm glad that I made it back during the previews. I tell you, there's nothing like a good movie to ease your day. "Hey, I brought the essentials." Turning to me smiling, Tammie reaches up for the popcorn.

"Wait a minute now. This is my popcorn."

Looking somewhat disappointed, "But I'm hungry."

"I'm not going to be mean and all. You can have some, but you're not getting the whole bag." Giving me that puppy dog look, I try my best to look unbothered. But how can you resist a smile like that. "Oh alright."

"Thanks."

Looking back at her now, "Yeah, yeah."

Heading back to the concession counter, my only thought is to make it back in time for the first five minutes. I have this five minute rule. If you don't make a movie in the first five minutes, you'll be completely clueless at the ending. So many movies bring their stories full circle. It's almost like the first five minutes is a model for the ending and its meaning.

Bump!

Looking up, I accidently bumped the woman in front of me. "Oh, I'm so, so sorry." Helping her wipe off the sporadic drops of coke on her shirt. Seeing that she's wearing a white top, I'm hoping that it doesn't stain. "Oh, I'm soooo sorry ma'am."

"It's fine. It's fine."

"Alright honey, here you go. I've got your famous popcorn topped with extra butter and—" looking me dead in the face, it's Gerald. Holding drinks, popcorn, and candy, he's just standing there eyes wide and mouth opened. Taking in the situation, I quickly figure out that this is his wife. Shocked beyond measure, I say nothing.

"Ahhh, baby thank you." Giving him a kiss softly on the cheek. She doesn't look old or washed up. She looks young, vibrant, and pretty. Looking at them together now, I notice something. Something that I didn't notice before hand. His wife has a little bump in her belly. . . .a baby bump. Wow, he's gotten her pregnant again. Just when I thought that he was going to leave her. Standing here, he acts like he doesn't even see me, like this is nothing. . . like I'm nothing to him. Realizing the place in which I stand, tears fill the wells of my eyes. Oh momma, ...oh momma, what do I do now?

"Well uh, what's going on here?" turning from her to me now, as if he's waiting for me to give some sort of explanation. But stuck in the moment, I've got nothing.

"Oh baby, I wasn't looking and I messed around and ran into her. Look, I messed up my shirt and everything."

With both of them laughing, I just stand still. Look at them. . . no, look at her. In her eyes, there's so much trust, so much hope, and so much love. "I'm going to go to the ladies' room and try to clean this up. I'll be back in a minute." Turning her attention to me. "Thank you sweetie."

"You're welcome." As she turns to leave, so do I . . . .going away, far away. . . . .anywhere but—

"What are you doing here?" breathes Gerald as he grabs my arm and slams me into the wall. Looking up and down the hallway now, we're the only ones here. He must have followed me, and deep in my feelings, I didn't even notice it.

"Let go of me. That hurts!"

"What are you doing here Bridgett? Trying to ruin my family?" looking at him now, I don't even recognize him.

"I told you to let go of me!" finally snatching my arm free. In the heat of the moment, hot wet tears roll down my face. He's still talking, but I've already tuned him out. I don't know what's gotten into him. With him doing all of this yelling and screaming, you would think that I'm his child or something. Looking in his eyes still, it's like there's nothing there. How can a man that shares my bed hurt me this way? How can someone who says that he loves me treat me so bad? If I really wanted to out him, I would have done it already. But, ...some things are better left alone. Smiling a little to myself, I just shake my head.

"Oh what, this is funny to you or something—"

"And what are you going to about it, huh? . . . .Are you going to hit me?" standing face to face with him now. I might have been a fool, but I will never be a victim. Surprising him a little, he backs up. Laughing to myself, well played Gerald. Well played. "You know, I remember my father. . .He was an old man with a young heart. . . .Ole' Robert, yeah I remember him. . ." leaning against the wall, it's like I feel the pain all over again.

Hearing footsteps down the hallway, it's Gerald's wife looking just as dense and confused. Turning to Gerald now, I can see that the macho man has left and the pleading coward has taken his place. The same eyes that were raging and mean are now begging me to keep my silence and keep his secrets. Ain't it funny how God turns the table! Not willing to give in, I step towards him and stand my ground.

"Yeah, you're just like Robert. A man for which enough. . . .is never enough." Seeing the confusion in her eyes, I can see that she's clueless. Should I tell her that her love, her one and only, is a lying-cheating bastard? Should I be the one to tell her that he stays out all time of night just so he doesn't have to come home? Should I be the one to tell her that husband is taking money from her household to support another woman? . . . . .Straightening up now, I'm about ready to lay everything out and in the open, but then. . . . .I hear momma's voice. . . . .singing to me. . . . .

". . . .pray on, pray on my child. . . . . pray. . . . . pray on my child. . . . I need you, to pray. . . . that the Lord will make a way. . . . pray on, pray on my child. . . . ."

Hearing momma's voice, it's like she always knows when to come. She always knew how to be the strength that I needed. Oh momma, I didn't understand way back when, but momma. . . . Oh momma, I understand it now.

With slow, wet tears traveling down my face, I just smile. Seeing the woman there, I can't break her heart with the truth. So instead, I continue to mask her lie. Stepping toward her, I embrace her, because out of all of us, she's going to need it. Stepping back now, boy does she looked surprised, but still I smile. "Thank you. . .You've helped me tonight more than you know."

"Oh you're welcome.. . .I guess." Looking at Gerald now, who's standing on pens and needles as is, she joins hands with him. . .as if to show me that that's her man. Don't worry, I don't want him. . . .not anymore.

"Well, have a nice day ma'am and congratulations on the baby." Still smiling, I start to walk away. "Bye." Not knowing what to say, she says nothing and neither does Gerald. But he didn't have to, because for the first time in my life, I'm free. Free to love, and free to be loved, by someone who'd actually care for me and mean it. I'm free, yes I'm free.

Getting back to my seat now, Tammie looks up at me with a guilty conscious. I haven't been gone but a few minutes and she's already half-way done with the bag. "What? You were gone so long and I got hungry ok."

"You're fine." I say, laughing in my seat.

"Where's the other popcorn?"

Still smiling, I turn to her. "It was too crowded out there. I'll get some later."

All through the movie, Gerald texts my phone non-stop. Doesn't he get it? I'm done with him. . . I can't hurt her anymore more. . . . no, not anymore. I've already said my good-bye, maybe it's time that he's said his. Leaving the theater, I can tell that a change is coming my way.

***

Momma Dee

Seeing my poor Bridgee, I pray that the Lord gives her peace. Maybe it's better this way. Maybe she's finally figured out. . . .that borrowed men can never stay.

Picking yet another rose from the basket whose petals are crying too, I just smile. As I bend down, I take the rose and stand it in the ground upright, so that the Lord will go ahead and make it bloom in plain sight.

Chapter 7:
June 16, 2015

Lamar

When I got out of jail, I knew that I had to do something fast. So day after day, I've been searching the classifieds and ripping through ads. I've got to get my life together, time ain't forever. I have to do this, because over the years, I've been a poor excuse of a big brother. I've allowed my sister to become a victim of the streets. I've single-handedly caused my two nephews to be raised by the state week after week. God, I have to make this right. So cheers to me for finally taking control of my life.

Walking the streets in the Summer time ain't no joke! I've been out here for hours, getting turned down at this place and that. It seems as if all of them have same long drawn out boring excuses, 'You have an extensive criminal record.' No joke, I haven't had a job in over 5 years. How else was I supposed to get money? 'You have limited work history.' Yeah well, that's kind of the reason why I'm applying for a job today. 'You didn't quite pass our drug test screening.' Shoot, I was going to need some kind of help to get through this.

Tired and frustrated, I plop down on the nearest park bench. Things can't get any worse even if they tried. Well momma, you can't say that I didn't try.

"Hey young man?" walking up behind me, it's Deacon Brown. Lord that's just what I need, another lecture on what young men my age should be doing. Not today Deac, . . . not today.

"Hey."

"Is this seat taken?"

"It's a free country." Shrugging my shoulders as he joins me on the bench.

"Today's a real good day. A hot day, but a good one. . . .It seems just perfect for fishing." Not really wanting to hear anything that he has to say, I simply turn my head and slouch further down in my seat. Man, I hope that I don't have to listen to this all day. "You know, I can remember the last time that I was out here, on a day much like this one. I wasn't quite your age though, I had to be about 16, if that. I had just left Mac' Daddy's Bar and Grill. It used to be down there on Patterson Street. That was my first job, but to tell you the truth, I hated that place. . ." caught up in the moment, he laughs at the mention of it.

"Well, if you hated it so much, why didn't you quit?"

"Oh I did! I was on dish duty that night, and the owner, Daddy J, came up to me just a fussing; you don't know him, he was before your time. He wasn't a very big man, but Lord knows that he was a rude one. He always wore suspenders high and tight, hat titled just right, cigar hanging in the corner of mouth, and fist full of whiskey in his flask. He cussed like a sailor and would stand toe to toe with any man. . . .Yeah, he was a character."

Watching him go down memory lane, I see something different in his eyes. All I've ever heard him talk about was church and the 'goodness of the Lord.' I've never heard him talk about his past before. Sitting here now, I don't know whether it's curiosity or just plain nosey but I've got to hear the rest of it. I mean, he can't just stop the story there. "Well. . . .what happened?"

"Oh, it was time for me get off, and boy was I ready! I had a pretty little young lady coming to see me that night. I had put on my finest clothes, combed my hair back, and even managed to get the keys to my father's car that night. Being young and broke at the time, I didn't have any money for flowers, so I picked some roses from our garden and tied them together."

"Oh, . . . " laughing out loud now. "I see where you were headed. Who knew that old Deac used to get his grove on!"

"Yeah well. . . . .let's just say that nothing happened as it should've that night. When I came out the back, my lady was waiting for me at the counter. Smiling and grinning, she was the prettiest girl that I'd ever seen. Trying to be a gentleman, I handed her the roses. She took one look at them and said, 'Boy don't tell me that you're this cheap. Garden Roses? I hope you know that you're going to have to come out of pocket with me. I'm not one of your usual chicks.' We both laughed it off, and that's when I picked up my father's keys and said, 'Woman, you better come with me before you be walking.' Laughing again, we got up and got ready to go. But just before we left, out comes Daddy J calling me every name in the book—"

"Why? What for?"

"I don't really remember. Daddy J was a crazy cat who stayed drunk all of the time. He was always fussing and fighting about something. I would usually take his crap with no complaints, but that night was a little different. I felt like I had something to prove that night. Embarrassed in front of my girl, I was in between a rock and a hard place. On one hand, I could take his crap like I always did and punch back in on the clock. While on the other hand, I could stand up to him and risk losing my job. At the time, I was the only one working in my house. My dad was a drunk. My momma was dead, and my sisters and brothers were still children. So you see, whether I wanted to admit it or not, I needed that job. So I swallowed my pride and went back into the kitchen doing things that Daddy J could've very well done himself. When I come out, I couldn't believe my eyes. . ." pausing for a moment, I can see his pain. "Out there in plain sight was Daddy J romancing my woman. Walking over to them, I asked her was she ready to go. But by the look on her face, I could tell that things had changed. She never even answered me, Daddy J did. With a cigar in his and hat titled to the side, he said 'Nah, I think a lady as pretty as this one deserves to be with a real man.' With a smile on his face, his took her by the hand and give me back the roses, . . . and I watched as the two of them walked out of the door. . ." with tears rolling down his face, I really don't know what to do. This man is over 50, and he's still hurt by something that happened when he was 16. Man, in his defense though, that was pretty messed up. ". . .Holding those bear roses, I felt each thorn. But I didn't care, because seeing her leave felt worse. . . .So I took off, and I came right here and sat on this bench. And I cried,

Lord knows I cried. I don't think that I ever felt for a woman as much as I did her. . ."

"So what happened next?"

"I quit Mac' Daddy's and I started working at the mine. I met someone else, got married, and had kids of my own. I loved my wife, but not like my first love. . . .I guess some things just aren't replaceable, to the heart anyway."

"What happened to the girl?"

"She dated Daddy J, who was twice her age, and had a baby for him, a little girl I believe. Not too long after that, they split."

"That's it. You don't know anything else about her?"

"No, but you do." Turning towards me, he just smiles. "She was your mother."

In complete shock, I can't do anything but stare at him. My momma was his crush. What? You've got to be kidding me. Well then, wait a minute that would mean that Daddy J is Sonya's father. Wow, momma you sure knew how to pick them! Looking at Deacon Brown now, I kind of feel sorry for him, but looking at things in retrospect, even though she was my mother and all, he probably dodged the bullet on that one.

"Man, it's a small world."

"That it is. . .So you see, change happens on this bench, whether you want it to or not. When I sat on this bench many years ago, I made the decision to leave my only form of employment and start life for myself."

"You did more than that. You closed the chapter to your pain. I guess it's true, 'all things do work together for the good of those who love the Lord.'"

"Whoo, whooo, your mother was a wonderful woman. She may have had some problems along the way, but she was a great woman and a great mother. She loved ya'll to death. . .It's like when I was holding that rose, it was beautiful but it still hurt because I knew what it stood for, a love that's been lost. Sitting here on this bench, I can tell that you're holding a rose of your own. Not a physical one but an emotional one. You can't see the beauty of life because you can't get past the pain of holding it together. You're family's a mess. Sonya's gone, Tammie's pregnant, Zectric and Tyrell are in foster care, Bridgett's out in the world, and you don't know what to do. Job 8:7 tells us that your latter days will be better than you're beginning. You're going through a Job experience right now where everything is falling apart, but Lamar . . . He who kneels before God can stand before any man. Come back to God and He *will* add all things unto you!"

Struggling to keep my own tears back, I just shake my head. "Well how am I supposed to do that? I can't get a job. I ain't got no money—"

"Boy if you've got God, you've got all that you need. Money won't solve anything. It's just a resource. God is your source. God is the one who supplies all of your needs. Go to God! Lamar listen, as a man, God has made you the head. If you want your family to fall in line, then you've got to take your place! Stop hustling on these street corners and start showing up at the house of God. Stop crying about your situation, and make some steps. Show God how bad you want it. You might not have a job right now, but I'm pretty sure that you know how to cut grass or wash a car. Stop waiting for the tides to be just right, and bloom where you're planted. Pick your head up and take your place!" feeling that he's gotten his point across, Deacon Brown gets up and leaves.

As I watch him walk away, I feel my strength coming back. And for the first time in a while, I feel that it's time to make a change!

***

June 19, 2015

Tammie

"Blow out the candles baby girl!" cheesing from ear to ear, its Bridgett.

Blowing out the candles, its official, I'm 13! Looking around the table, it's just Bridgett, Lamar, and I. And to be honest, I'm kind of glad that it's just us three. It's been a long time since we've sat at the dinner table together. . . a long time.

"So birthday girl, what did you wish for?" asks Lamar.

"I'm not telling."

"Why not?"

"'Cause if I do, it want come true."

"Ok well be that way then."

"Ok would you two just chill out for a minute and taste this cake. I made it and I need some test tasters to tell me how I did?" looking at us both.

"Wait, you mean to tell me that you didn't taste your own cake?" laughing to myself, you can always count on Lamar to bring out the obvious.

"Uhhh no, that's why I need ya'll." Pushing the cake over to us, Bridgett smiles in expectancy. My Lord, I love my sister to death, but You know that she can't even boil water. Looking at Lamar, I'm trying my best to get him to go first, but with one smirk, he just shakes his head.

"Ladies first." Now how did I know that he was going to push me up to do this! Taking a deep breath, I cut me a small piece not wanting to hurt my sister's feelings. As I take the first bite, all eyes are on me.

"Well, tell me. How'd I do?" smiling from cheek to cheek as if her eyes are trying to coerce me to say something in her favor.

"Tammie just lay it on the line, she can't cook!"

"Shut-up Lamar. At least I'm trying!" watching the two of them fuss and agree, I can't help but laugh. Good times, good times.

Ring! Ring!

"I'll get it." Says Lamar as he gets up from his chair. While he's over there getting that, I'll just finish my cake.

"Mmmm, I see that somebody's feeling my cake!"

"Yeah, it tastes alright, . . . but you still can't cook!" with us both laughing now, things seem to be going pretty great.

"Hey, ya'll will never believe who I just got off the phone with!" coming in all out of breath, Bridget and I are clueless. But overly excited, Lamar keeps talking anyway. "Family and Children Services. It seems as if our appeal has been approved. Tyrell and Zectric are coming home!"

"Oh my God!" with the three of us up now, we're jumping, hugging, crying, and cheering. Thank you Lord for being on our side!

Chapter 8:
August 22, 2015

Bridgett

"God has. . . .smiled on me. He has set me freeeee.. . . God has. . . oh yea, smiled on me. . .He's been gooooood. . . to meeeeee. God has. . . .yes He has, smiled on me. . . He has set me freeeeeee. . .God has. . . .smiled on meeeee. . . .He's been gooood to meeeee—"

"Man Auntie what's all that fuss? Some of us are still trying to sleep." Turning back, it's Zectric coming down the stairs just as sleepy as he wants to be. Shooting him a quick grin, I continue to stir my grits.

"Boy don't you know music when you hear it? Besides, it's about time that you got up. I'm almost done with breakfast."

Taking his seat to the table, he lets out a deep sigh. "Ahhhhh auntie! You don't have to kill me yet. I'll just eat cereal."

Turning back to him sharply, "Boy, I can cook. You're not going to eat any cereal. You're going to sit right there and eat what I've been preparing all morning."

"Oh alright, what all is it?"

"Grits, eggs, biscuits, and bacon." Smiling back at him, quite pleased with myself. "You'll love it."

"Let's hope so."

"Where's Tammie and Tyrell?"

"They're still sleep."

"Yeah well, in a minute I'm going to need you to get them up so that they can get ready for school too." Placing a plate of food before him. "Here you go sweetie."

Giving me those slick eyes, he slowly pulls the plate closer to him. I don't know where everyone in this family gets the notion that I'm such a terrible cook. I mean, I burn one pot of noodles and my reputation is shot to the creek.

Knock! Knock!

Saved by the bell, he leaps up from his chair and heads for the door. "I'll get it." As he goes to the door, I decide that it's time to get the others up as well. I'm not trying to be caught up in that morning traffic again.

"Tammie! Terrell! Ya'll get up. I'm not being late this morning! Get up!" I yell from the bottom of the steps. Stumbling to her doorway, I see Tammie as she peeps her head out.

"Okay, ok already. I'll be down in a minute."

"I hear you baby sis. Give me five minutes." Yarns Lamar on his way to Tyrell's room. Good. He'll make sure that he's up for me.

Turning back to the kitchen now, "Zectric baby come on and finish your brea---" stopping dead in my tracks, I see a ghost of a man in front of me. Gerald! No freaking way. What in the world is he doing here?

Seeing Zectric ease his way to his chair, I'm not really sure of what to say. He's just a child. He doesn't need to hear all of this. "Zectric baby, can you go upstairs and make sure that Tyrell's up for me?"

"Ok." And with that he walks half-way up the stairs. "Tyrell! Auntie said get up." Coming back down the steps, he sits back down at the table like his job is done.

Looking at him now, I can't do anything but laugh. That's Zectric alright. "Zectric take yourself upstairs."

"Why? I haven't even finished my breakfast."

"And you won't if you don't make it up those steps."

"Oh alright." Stomping his feet in frustration, he makes it up three steps and sits down.

"Zectric!"

"What? You told me to go up the steps. You never said how far."

"All the way up the steps, now go!" taking a deep sigh, he finally makes his way to his room. Still laughing, I turn back to Gerald.

"Well, he seems to be one for jokes this morning." Trying his best to ease the tension.

"What are you doing here Gerald?"

"I've been calling you, texting you, and I even went by the apartment. You've moved all of your stuff out. I mean, what is this? What's going on?"

Staring at him now, it's like he doesn't even think that that night at the movies even happened. How in the world does he think that he's going to come back from that? "Go home Gerald. It's over—"

"Now Bridgett, wait a minute. You can't just—"

"It's over! We and whatever else that was going on is over. Done. Finished. Kaput . How many ways do you want me to say it?" looking at him now, I can see him getting angrier by the minute.

Lunging towards me, he grabs me by my arm again like he's lost all form of control.

"Let go of me. Let go—"

"Is there a problem here?" coming down the stairs, its Lamar followed by Tammie and the boys, each one looking in horror.

Letting go of my arm and straightening up his face, Gerald takes a few steps back. "No, nothing at all just a little friendly conver—"

"It doesn't look friendly." Walking down the steps and towards the door, Lamar pulls the door open. "I believe that my sister was asking you to leave."

"We're not done talking---"

"Yeah well I'm ending it. It's time for you to leave." As he spoke with such authority, I didn't even recognize him. Standing there all stern and serious, I'm not sure that Gerald knows how to take him either, so instead of fighting the issue, he just leaves. And just like that, Gerald walks out of my life. This time for good.

Closing the front door, Lamar walks over to the table and sits down. Nobody's moving, we're just staring at him in full shock. Looking up at us, Lamar just smiles. "Are ya'll going to stand there all day?"

With everyone laughing, we all head back to the table as well.

"Uncle Lamar you almost had that man for lunch." Says Zectric, too excited to finish his plate.

"Yeah well, what can I say? I'm a man like that." Laughing just as silly as ever. "Come on ya'll let's say grace."

"Since when we do that? You've been doing that a lot lately." asks Zectric.

"Oh don't ask. Lamar's been on a Jesus trip for a long time now. He's even dragged us to church during the week-long revival back in June." Explains Tammie.

Shaking his head in shock, Tyrell just smiles. "Boy, boy if Momma Dee could see you now. She'll be rolling over in her grave backgrounds." With everyone laughing again, I have to agree with Tyrell, momma would be surprised. Not just at Lamar, but of all of us. Who knew that it would've taken all of this?

September 11, 2015

Lamar

Boy I tell you, working on cars all day long makes you more tired than a little bit, but hey, at least I get off in time enough to pick up the boys. So, hands dirty and all, I pull up to the school in my little hooptie. It's nothing to brag about, just something to get around. I got it at the shop for a good deal. It's an '07 Honda Civic, but it runs like a trooper. Pulling up to the school, I sit in the car and wait for the children to get out.

Man, life has been one wild ride. With me and Bridgett both working, we've been able to pay down Momma's debt. Tammie's walking around here like she's about to pop any day now, so we've finally cleared out momma's room and made it into a nursery. Not really wanting to put momma's stuff just anywhere, we put most of the things in the attic.

Ding! Ding! Ding!

Hearing the bell ring, I sit up and watch as children come out the building faster than a swarm of bees. Getting out of the car, I spot Zectric who's dragging Tyrell by the hand. Spotting me, he waves like there's no tomorrow. Laughing to myself, I wave back.

Just as they step off of the curb, I spot a familiar face get out of an SUV and grab them. Realizing what's going on,

I run up there to stop her. "Hey, hey. What are you doing Sonya?"

Turning back toward me, she's clearly surprised. Standing up now, "Oh Lamar, hey how are you?" stepping forward to hug me. Shocked myself, I step back. Was she really about to take the boys?

"Sonya what are you doing here? Were you about to take them? Just like that?"

"Well uh, Kyle. ." motioning to the guy in the truck, whose obviously her new man. . .sucker husband #3. ". . .he and I have this place down South, and I wouldn't dare dream of going that far without my mini-me's." smiling from ear to ear like everything's alright. "You know?"

"No . . .I really don't. You pack up and leave in the middle of the night. Now you want to come back like everything's alright."

Getting irritated, she just turns her head. "Look, I don't need a lecture. Especially not from you. . ." grabbing the boys, "I just want to get my kids and go."

"Wait a minute, your kids? Oh, I forgot to tell you. . .The state took custody of them a few months back. With no parent to contest it, the state gave custody to Bridgett and I. . . So,. . ." pulling the boys back, ". . .we've adopted them."

"Adopted them? Wait, what are you saying?"

"I'm saying that legally, you're not their mother anymore. Bridgett and I have all of the parental rights. So you can get back in the truck and go wherever you have to go, but they're not coming with you." Standing firm with Zectric on my left and Tyrell on my right, I can see that Sonya's shocked, maybe even hurt. Standing in front of me with tears in her eyes, she shakes her head in disbelief.

"No, no, you can't take my babies. . ." bending down now in front of them. "You're my boys. You're my babies. I'm your mot—"

"No you're not! Momma Dee was my momma." Looking down at Zectric now, I'm stunned myself.

Following up behind Zectric, Tyrell steps forward. "Yeah, and we're not going with you. We're staying with Uncle and Auntie in *our* house."

Stepping back like she's lost her best friend, Sonya doesn't know what to do.

"Look, you know where to find us." Turning to the boys now, "Come on ya'll let's go." Watching us walk away, it's like she's dying right there on the street with no air to breathe, but nobody cares anymore. . . .not even me.

***

Momma Dee

Standing here looking at my children trying their best to get along. Who knew that God would have to move me just to get them used to living on their own. Working as a team, they pull strength from one another, I'm just so glad that they stuck together through the struggle. Bridgett has come home, the prodigal child that has returned. And Lamar has chosen to stand as a man knowing that all respect must be earned. Tammie has chosen to see the beauty within herself and has finally accepted the situation that is to be. Surrounded by so much support, she knows that everything will work out just fine.

But poor Sonya, my oldest child who has gone astray. She's so much like her father, a miniature Daddy J. I hope she knows that nothing in life comes free. Living is a struggle every day of the week.

Lord I thank you for all that I went through, because had I not done those things, my children wouldn't have known what to do. Walking away, I'm still holding the basket tightly in my hand. Looking at the roses now, I see no more tears, no more falling petals. Now I can go home and finally rest. . .free to drop my basket and allow all of the roses to bloom where that bloom best.

www.ingramcontent.com/pod-product-compliance
Lightning Source LLC
Chambersburg PA
CBHW050042080526
44586CB00014B/1425